Las Vegas

Travel Guide

2023 - 2024

A First Time Travelers
Guide| The Ultimate Las
Vegas Travel Guide 2023 to
Explore the City's Best
Sights, Activities, and
Restaurants|Most
Recent|2023 updated|2024
updated

Nate Knight

Copyright

Table of Contents

Introduction

Las Vegas is a city of dreams, where anything is possible. It's a place where you can gamble your heart out, see the world's best shows, and eat at some of the finest restaurants. But there's more to Las Vegas than just gambling and shows. There are also plenty of family-friendly activities, such as visiting the High Roller Observation Wheel or the Shark Reef Aquarium.

No matter what you're looking for in a vacation, Las Vegas has something to offer. So what are you waiting for? Start planning your trip today!

Here are some of the things that make Las Vegas a great place to visit:
- The casinos
- The shows
- The restaurants
- The nightlife
- The family-friendly activities

If you're looking for a vacation that's full of excitement and adventure, Las Vegas is the perfect place for you. Start planning your trip today!

About Las Vegas

Las Vegas is a city in the Mojave Desert in the U.S. state of Nevada. It is known for its casinos, hotels, and entertainment. The city is home to the Las Vegas Strip, a stretch of hotels and casinos along the Las Vegas Boulevard South. The Strip is home to some of the world's most famous casinos, including the Bellagio, the Venetian, and the Caesars Palace.

Las Vegas is also home to a variety of other attractions, including the Fremont Street Experience, a pedestrian mall with light shows and street performers; the High Roller, the world's tallest Ferris wheel; and the Stratosphere Tower, which offers panoramic views of the city.

Planning Your Trip

The best time to visit Las Vegas is during the spring (March-May) or fall (September-November). The weather is mild during these months, and there are fewer crowds. If you are planning to visit during the summer (June-August), be prepared for hot and humid weather.

There are many ways to get to Las Vegas. The city is served by McCarran International Airport, which is located just outside of the city center. There are also several bus lines that travel to Las Vegas from other major cities.

Once you arrive in Las Vegas, you can get around the city by taxi, Uber, or Lyft. There is also a public bus system, but it is not as extensive as the taxi or ride-hailing services.

Getting to Las Vegas

Las Vegas is easily accessible by air, car, or bus.

- **By air:** McCarran International Airport (LAS) is the main airport serving Las Vegas. It is located about 10 miles (16 kilometers) from the Las Vegas Strip. There are many airlines that fly to LAS from major cities around the world.

- **By car:** Las Vegas is located on Interstate 15, which connects it to Los Angeles, Salt Lake City, and Phoenix. There are also several major highways that connect Las Vegas to other cities in Nevada.

- By bus: Greyhound and Megabus offer bus service to Las Vegas from many major cities.

Getting Around Las Vegas

The best way to get around Las Vegas is by taxi, Uber, or Lyft. There is also a public bus system, but it is not as extensive as the taxi or ride-hailing services.

If you are staying on the Las Vegas Strip, you can easily walk between most of the hotels and casinos. However, if you are staying off the Strip, you will need to use public transportation or a taxi to get around.

Must-See Attractions in Kos Vegas

The Las Vegas Strip

This is a must-see for any visitor to Las Vegas. This iconic stretch of hotels and casinos is home to some of the most famous casinos in the world, including the Bellagio, the Venetian, and the Caesars Palace. The Strip is also home to a variety of other attractions, such as the High Roller Observation Wheel, the Eiffel Tower Viewing Deck, and the Stratosphere Tower.

Fremont Street Experience

This is a pedestrian mall located in downtown Las Vegas. The Experience features a light show that runs every 15 minutes, as well as street performers and other entertainment.

Bellagio Conservatory & Botanical Garden

This is a stunning garden located in the Bellagio hotel. The garden is home to a variety of flowers and plants, as well as a variety of art installations.

High Roller Observation Wheel

This is the world's tallest Ferris wheel. The wheel offers panoramic views of Las Vegas and the surrounding area.

Eiffel Tower Viewing Deck

This is located at the top of the Eiffel Tower replica in Paris Las Vegas. The deck offers stunning views of the Las Vegas Strip and the surrounding area.

Stratosphere Tower

This is the tallest freestanding tower in the United States. The tower offers panoramic views of Las Vegas and the surrounding area.

Madame Tussauds Las Vegas

This is a wax museum featuring lifelike wax figures of celebrities, historical figures, and other notable people.

The Venetian

This is a luxury hotel and casino modeled after Venice, Italy. The hotel features a replica of St. Mark's Square and a Grand Canal that guests can take a gondola ride on.

The Mirage Volcano

This is an erupting volcano located in front of the Mirage hotel. The volcano erupts every 15 minutes and is accompanied by sound and light effects.

Mandalay Bay Shark Reef Aquarium

This is a 1.5 million gallon aquarium that features sharks, rays, and other marine life.

The Mob Museum

This is a museum dedicated to the history of organized crime in the United States. The museum features exhibits on the Mafia, the Las Vegas Outfit, and other criminal organizations.

These are just a few of the many must-see attractions in Las Vegas. With so much to see and do, you're sure to have an unforgettable time in Sin City.

Things to Do In Los Vegas

Visit a casino

Las Vegas is known for its casinos, so it's a must-do for any visitor. There are casinos of all sizes and themes, so you're sure to find one that you'll enjoy.

See a show

Las Vegas is home to some of the best shows in the world, from Broadway musicals to magic shows to comedy acts. There's something for everyone, so be sure to check out the show schedule before you go.

Go shopping

Las Vegas is a shopper's paradise. There are malls, outlet stores, and boutique shops to explore. You can find everything from designer clothes to souvenirs to electronics.

Eat at a celebrity chef restaurant

Las Vegas is home to many celebrity chef restaurants, such as Gordon Ramsay's Hell's Kitchen and Bobby Flay's Mesa Grill. These restaurants offer high-quality food and a dining experience that you won't forget.

Take a helicopter tour

A helicopter tour is a great way to see the sights of Las Vegas from a bird's-eye view. You can see the Strip, the Grand Canyon, and even Death Valley.

Red Rock Canyon National Conservation Area

Red Rock Canyon is a beautiful natural area located just outside of Las Vegas. There are trails for all levels of hikers and bikers.

Visit the Neon Museum

The Neon Museum is a non-profit organization that collects and preserves historic Las Vegas neon signs. The museum offers tours of the signs, which are a fascinating glimpse into the history of Las Vegas.

Take a day trip to Death Valley National Park

Death Valley is the hottest and driest national park in the United States. It's a unique and fascinating place to visit, and it's only a few hours from Las Vegas.

Visit the Hoover Dam

The Hoover Dam is a massive dam that straddles the border between Nevada and Arizona. It's a popular tourist destination, and it offers stunning views of the Colorado River.

These are just a few of the many things to do in Las Vegas. With so much to see and do, you're sure to have an unforgettable time in Sin City.

Here are some other family-friendly activities in Las Vegas:

- Visit the High Roller Observation Wheel

- See the Bellagio Conservatory & Botanical Garden

- Take a ride on the Fremont Street Experience

- Visit the Shark Reef Aquarium at Mandalay Bay

- Play mini-golf at Topgolf Las Vegas

Where to Stay in Los Vegas

Luxury Hotels

- **The Bellagio**
  Tnis is a 5-star hotel and casino located on the Las Vegas Strip. The hotel is known for its beautiful gardens, its world-class restaurants, and its famous water fountain show.

- **The Venetian**
  this is a luxury hotel and casino that is modeled after Venice, Italy. The hotel features a replica of St. Mark's Square and a Grand Canal that guests can take a gondola ride on.

- **The Wynn**
  This is a luxury hotel and casino located on the Las Vegas Strip. The hotel is known for its

luxurious accommodations, its award-winning spas, and its stunning views of the Strip.

- **The Cosmopolitan of Las Vegas**
  This is a luxury hotel and casino located on the Las Vegas Strip. The hotel is known for its trendy restaurants, its lively nightlife, and its rooftop pool with views of the Strip.

- *Mandalay Bay*
  This is a luxury hotel and casino located on the Las Vegas Strip. The hotel is known for its Shark Reef Aquarium, its lazy river, and its concert venue.

Family-Friendly Hotels

- *Caesars Palace*
  This is a family-friendly hotel and casino located on the Las

Vegas Strip. The hotel features a variety of attractions for kids, including a water park, a roller coaster, and a Roman Forum.

- **The Mirage**
  This is a family-friendly hotel and casino located on the Las Vegas Strip. The hotel features a volcano that erupts every 15 minutes, a dolphin habitat, and a tropical garden.

- **The Palms**
  This is a family-friendly hotel and casino located on the Las Vegas Strip. The hotel features a bowling alley, an arcade, and a movie theater.

Budget-Friendly Hotels

- **Excalibur**

This is a budget-friendly hotel and casino located on the Las Vegas Strip. The hotel features a medieval theme, a jousting tournament, and a pool with pirate ships.

- **The STRAT Hotel, Casino & Tower**
  This is a budget-friendly hotel and casino located on the Las Vegas Strip. The hotel features a thrill ride that takes you 1,081 feet above the city, as well as a casino and a bowling alley.

- *Gold Coast Hotel and Casino*
  This is a budget-friendly hotel and casino located off the Las Vegas Strip. The hotel features a casino, a spa, and a pool.

These are just a few of the many great places to stay in Las Vegas. When choosing a hotel, consider your budget, your interests, and the location that is most convenient for you.

Where to Eat In Los Vegas

Celebrity Chef Restaurants

- **Guy Fieri's Vegas Kitchen & Bar**

  This is a casual restaurant with a menu that features Guy Fieri's signature dishes, such as the Bacon Mac Bites and the Big Bite Burger.

- **Gordon Ramsay Hell's Kitchen**

  This is a fine dining restaurant where you can watch the chefs compete in the same kitchen as the TV show. The menu features modern American cuisine with a Mediterranean twist.

- **The Eiffel Tower Restaurant**

It offers stunning views of the Las Vegas Strip from its 1,073-foot perch. The menu features classic French cuisine with a modern twist.

- **Jean-Georges Steakhouse**
  This is a fine dining steakhouse that offers dry-aged steaks, seafood, and classic French dishes.

Buffets

- **The Cosmopolitan's Wicked Spoon Buffet**
  This is a popular buffet with a wide variety of dishes, including sushi, carving stations, and desserts.

- **The Mirage's VooDoo Steakhouse**
  It offers a buffet with a New Orleans theme. The menu

features Creole and Cajun dishes, as well as seafood and steaks.

- **Caesars Palace's Bacchanal Buffet**
  It is one of the largest buffets in Las Vegas. The menu features over 500 dishes, including sushi, carving stations, and desserts.

Other Restaurants

- **The Venetian's Grand Canal Shoppes**
  This is a food hall with over 30 restaurants, including Wolfgang Puck's Spago and The Cheesecake Factory.

- **Mandalay Bay's Shark Reef Aquarium Restaurant**
  It offers a unique dining experience with views of the

aquarium. The menu features seafood dishes and sushi.

- **The Palms' Nectar**
  This is a rooftop restaurant with stunning views of the Las Vegas Strip. The menu features California cuisine with a modern twist.

- **The Stratosphere's Top of the World**
  This is a revolving restaurant with 360-degree views of Las Vegas. The menu features American cuisine with a Southwestern twist.

These are just a few of the many great places to eat in Las Vegas. When choosing a restaurant, consider your budget, your dietary restrictions, and your taste preferences.

Shopping

The Forum Shops at Caesars Palace

This is an upscale shopping mall located on the Las Vegas Strip. The mall features over 160 stores, including Gucci, Prada, and Louis Vuitton.

The Venetian Grand Canal Shoppes

This is a shopping mall that is modeled after Venice, Italy. The mall features over 160 stores, as well as a replica of St. Mark's Square and a Grand Canal that guests can take a gondola ride on.

Fashion Show Mall

This is the largest shopping mall in Las Vegas. The mall features over 250 stores, including Macy's, Nordstrom, and Dillard's.

Premium Outlets Las Vegas

This is a factory outlet mall located just off the Las Vegas Strip. The mall features over 150 stores, including Coach, Nike, and Michael Kors.

These are just a few of the many great places to shop in Las Vegas. When choosing a shopping destination, consider your budget, your interests, and the location that is most convenient for you.

Here are some additional tips for shopping in Las Vegas:

- Shop during the week to avoid the crowds.
- Look for coupons and discounts. Many stores offer discounts to locals or to members of the military.
- Take advantage of outlet malls. Outlet malls offer discounts on name-brand merchandise.

- Don't be afraid to haggle. Many merchants are willing to negotiate prices, especially on high-end items.

Nightlife

Hyde Bellagio

This is a nightclub located at the Bellagio hotel and casino. The club is known for its VIP bottle service and its celebrity clientele.

Tao Nightclub

This is a nightclub located at the Venetian hotel and casino. The club is known for its Asian-inspired decor and its high-energy atmosphere.

XS Nightclub

This is a nightclub located at the Wynn hotel and casino. The club is known for its over-the-top production values and its celebrity DJs.

Marquee Nightclub

This is a nightclub located at the Cosmopolitan hotel and casino. The club is known for its massive dance floor and its state-of-the-art sound system.

Light Nightclub

This is a nightclub located at the Mandalay Bay hotel and casino. The club is known for its colorful laser light shows and its EDM music.

Omnia Nightclub

This is a nightclub located at Caesars Palace hotel and casino. The club is known for its rotating dance floor and its views of the Las Vegas Strip.

1 OAK Nightclub

This is a nightclub located at the Mirage hotel and casino. The club is known for its hip-hop music and its celebrity sightings.

Rain Nightclub

This is a nightclub located at the Palms hotel and casino. The club is known for its swimming pool parties and its VIP cabanas.

The View

This is a nightclub located at the Stratosphere hotel and casino. The club offers 360-degree views of Las Vegas and is open 24 hours a day.

Zouk Nightclub

This is a nightclub located at Resorts World Las Vegas. The club is known for its Asian-inspired decor and its high-energy atmosphere.

Hakkasan Las Vegas

This is a nightclub located at the MGM Grand hotel and casino. The club is known for its award-winning mixologists and its Asian-inspired cuisine.

These are just a few of the many great places to party in Las Vegas. When choosing a nightclub, consider your budget, your music preferences, and your desired atmosphere.

Here are some additional tips for clubbing in Las Vegas:

- Make a reservation. Many nightclubs require reservations, especially on weekends.

- Dress to impress. Nightclubs in Las Vegas have a dress code, so make sure you dress appropriately.

- Bring your ID. You will need your ID to get into most nightclubs.

- Be prepared to pay a cover charge. Cover charges can vary depending on the nightclub and the night of the week.

- Have fun! Las Vegas is a city that is all about having fun, so let loose and enjoy yourself.

Tips for Planning Your Las Vegas Trip

How to Book Your Las Vegas Trip

- Book your flights and hotel early. Las Vegas is a popular tourist destination, so prices can go up quickly.

- Consider booking a package deal. Package deals can often save you money on your flights, hotel, and activities.

- Be flexible with your dates. If you can, be flexible with your travel dates. This can help you get the best deals on flights and hotels.

- Consider staying off the Las Vegas Strip. There are many great hotels and resorts off the

Las Vegas Strip that offer more affordable rates.

- Book your activities in advance. Many popular activities in Las Vegas sell out quickly, so it's a good idea to book them in advance.

What to Pack for Your Las Vegas Trip

- Comfortable shoes. You'll be doing a lot of walking in Las Vegas, so make sure you pack comfortable shoes.

- Swimsuit. If you're planning on spending time at the pool or beach, be sure to pack a swimsuit.

- Dressy clothes. There are many nice restaurants and nightclubs in Las Vegas, so you'll want to pack some dressy clothes.

- Casual clothes. You'll also want to pack some casual clothes for exploring the city and going to shows.

- Hat and sunglasses. The sun can be strong in Las Vegas, so be sure to pack a hat and sunglasses to protect yourself.

- Sunscreen. Don't forget the sunscreen! The sun can be very strong in Las Vegas, so it's important to protect your skin.

Budgeting for Your Las Vegas Trip

- Estimate your costs. Before you start booking anything, take some time to estimate your costs. This will help you avoid overspending.

- Set a budget. Once you have an estimate of your costs, set a budget for your trip. This will help you stay on track financially.

- Be prepared to spend more. Las Vegas is a city of excess, so be prepared to spend more than you might expect.

- Look for ways to save money. There are many ways to save money in Las Vegas, such as booking a package deal, staying off the Las Vegas Strip, and eating at budget-friendly restaurants.

Things to know before you go

- The legal drinking age in Las Vegas is 21. Be prepared to show your ID if you want to purchase alcohol.

- The currency in Las Vegas is the US dollar. You can exchange your currency at most banks and currency exchange bureaus.

- Las Vegas is a very casual city, but there are some dress codes for certain restaurants and nightclubs. It's always best to err on the side of caution and dress more formally.

- Tipping is expected in Las Vegas. The standard tipping rate is 15-20%.

- Las Vegas is a very safe city, but it's always important to be aware of your surroundings. Be sure to keep your valuables close to you and don't walk alone at night.

Tipping etiquette

- Tipping is expected in Las Vegas. The standard tipping rate is 15-20%.

- Tipping your server is customary in restaurants. You can also tip your bellhop, valet, and room service attendant.

- If you're gambling, it's customary to tip the dealer. The amount of the tip is up to you, but a few dollars is usually sufficient.

- Tipping is not expected at most tourist attractions. However, you may want to tip your tour guide or driver if you feel they have provided excellent service.

Dress code

- Las Vegas is a very casual city, but there are some dress codes for certain restaurants and nightclubs. It's always best to err on the side of caution and dress more formally.

- Men should wear pants and a collared shirt. Women should wear skirts or dresses that are at least knee-length.

- Some nightclubs have a more strict dress code. You may be required to wear high heels or a dress.

- If you're not sure what to wear, it's always best to ask the restaurant or nightclub ahead of time.

Drinking age

- The legal drinking age in Las Vegas is 21. Be prepared to show your ID if you want to purchase alcohol.

- There are a few exceptions to the drinking age law. For example, people under 21 can drink alcohol if they are with their parents or legal guardians.

- It is illegal to drink and drive in Las Vegas. The legal blood alcohol concentration (BAC) limit is 0.08%.

Currency exchange

- The currency in Las Vegas is the US dollar. You can exchange your currency at most banks and currency exchange bureaus.

- The exchange rate will vary depending on the bank or

bureau. It's always a good idea to compare rates before you exchange your currency.

- Be sure to have some US dollars on hand when you arrive in Las Vegas. Many businesses do not accept foreign currency.

Safety tips

- Las Vegas is a very safe city, but it's always important to be aware of your surroundings. Be sure to keep your valuables close to you and don't walk alone at night.

- Don't accept drinks from strangers. There have been cases of people being drugged at bars and nightclubs.

- If you feel unsafe, don't hesitate to call the police. The Las Vegas Metropolitan Police Department can be reached at 911.

Printed in Great Britain
by Amazon

29668796R00030